Circular
Movement

by Lola M. Schaefer

Consulting Editor: Gail Saunders-Smith, Ph.D.

Consultant: P. W. Hammer, Ph.D., Acting Manager
of Education, American Institute of Physics

Pebble Books

an imprint of Capstone Press
Mankato, Minnesota

Pebble Books are published by Capstone Press
818 North Willow Street, Mankato, Minnesota 56001
http://www.capstone-press.com

Library of Congress Cataloging-in-Publication Data
Schaefer, Lola M., 1950–
    Circular movement/by Lola M. Schaefer.
    p. cm.—(The way things move)
    Includes bibliographical references and index.
    Summary: Simple text and photographs show objects that move in circles.
    ISBN 0-7368-0400-5
    1. Rotational motion—Juvenile literature. [1. Motion.] I. Title. II. Series.
QC133.5.S33   2000
531′.34—dc21   99-19414
                                                                      CIP

Note to Parents and Teachers

The series The Way Things Move supports national science standards for units on understanding motion and the principles that explain it. The series also shows that things move in many different ways. This book describes and illustrates circular movements. The photographs support emergent readers in understanding the text. The repetition of words and phrases helps emergent readers learn new words. This book also introduces emergent readers to subject-specific vocabulary words, which are defined in the Words to Know section. Emergent readers may need assistance to read some words and to use the Table of Contents, Words to Know, Read More, Internet Sites, and Index/Word List sections of the book.

Table of Contents

4

Circular movement is motion in a circle.

Merry-go-rounds move
in circles.

Windmill blades move in circles.

Seth Thomas

MADE IN USA

10

Clock hands move
in circles.

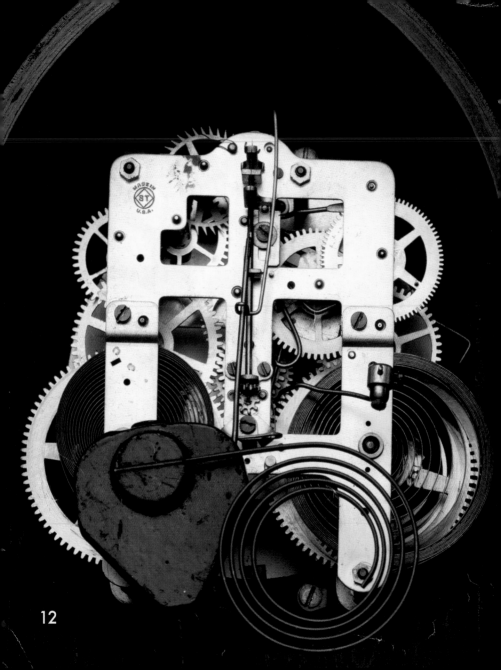

Gears move in circles.

Airplane propellers move in circles.

16

Ice skaters move in circles.

Hands move in circles.

People move in circles.

Words to Know

blade—a long, thin metal part; the wind pushes windmill blades in circles.

circle—a perfectly round shape; when things move in circles, they start and end at the same place.

gears—a set of wheels with teeth that fit together; gears move in circles to run machines.

merry-go-round—a ride with seats shaped like horses and other animals; people sit on the animals as the merry-go-round moves in a circle.

movement—the act of changing position from place to place

propeller—a set of blades that move in a circle; the movement of a propeller helps push a vehicle forward.

Read More

Dixon, Malcolm and Karen Smith. *Forces and Movement.* Young Scientists. Mankato, Minn.: Smart Apple Media, 1998.

Hindley, Judy. *The Wheeling and Whirling-Around Book.* Read and Wonder. Cambridge, Mass.: Candlewick Press, 1994.

Rau, Dana Meachen. *Circle City.* Rookie Reader. New York: Children's Press, 2000.

Internet Sites

From Windmills to Whirligigs
http://www.sci.mus.mn.us/sln/vollis

You Can Do It: Build a Windmill
http://www.looklearnanddo.com/documents/
sea_breeze_project.html

Index/Word List

Word Count: 43
Early-Intervention Level: 5

Editorial Credits
Martha E. H. Rustad, editor; Timothy Halldin, cover designer; Heidi Schoof, photo researcher

Photo Credits
Index Stock Imagery, 16
International Stock/John Bechtold, 12
Photri-Microstock/Tom McCarthy, 18
Richard Cummins, 1
Telegraph Colour Library/FPG International LLC, cover
Unicorn Stock Photos/Dennis Thompson, 14; Karen Holsinger Mullen, 20
Uniphoto, 10; Uniphoto/Terry Wild Studio, 4
Visuals Unlimited/Mark E. Gibson, 6; Larry Blank, 8